KNOW YOUR GAME:

Soccer

MARC BLOOM

SCHOLASTIC INC.
New York Toronto London Auckland Sydney

Acknowledgment

Special thanks to coaches Ron Greaux and Joe Santos, soccer experts who thrive on bringing out the best in young athletes.

ISBN 0-590-44315-6

Design: Brian Collins
Illustrations: Joe Taylor

Designed and produced by Peter Elek Associates,
457 Broome Street, New York, NY 10013

12 11 10 9 8 7 6 5 4 3 2 1   0 1 2 3 4 5/9

Printed in the U.S.A.   23

First Scholastic printing, August 1990

Contents

Introduction

Soccer is the world's most popular game. It is played in more than 150 countries by millions of people of all ages. In the United States alone, there are an estimated 10 million people involved in soccer as players, coaches, and referees.

One reason for soccer's popularity is that it is so much fun to play. Soccer gives you a chance to use your body, learn new skills, be active with friends, and play on a team.

This book will help you to enjoy soccer. It will explain how soccer is played and show you how to do your best at it.

You may already know a little bit about soccer. Maybe you've played with friends in someone's backyard, or are even a member of a soccer team. At one time, you may have watched a professional soccer match on television.

No matter what you know about soccer, there is much more to learn. The more you know about the game, the more you'll improve and the better you'll like it.

In this book, you'll read about soccer skills, rules, gear, and teamwork. You'll find out how to get in shape for soccer, how to set goals for yourself, and build up your confidence.

Soccer is a game almost anyone can play. Each person should have the chance to participate, learn, succeed—and enjoy playing soccer.

Chapter 1

Having Fun

Have you ever run around with a group of friends in a backyard or park? That's what soccer is like. It's an organized way to keep active, play with friends, and have fun.

When you play soccer, it's important to keep fun in mind. Most people your age play sports for this reason.

Having fun means feeling good about yourself. It also means knowing you tried your best. After a game, whether your team won or lost, you should be able to say to yourself, "I enjoyed the game, and I did my best."

Soccer can be fun for many different reasons. These reasons include: being a member of a team, learning sportsmanship, developing skills, getting healthful exercise, and playing with rules. Also, it's fun having a coach, increasing your self-confidence, and feeling proud to wear an athletic uniform.

Being a Member of a Team

A team is like a club. When you join a soccer team, you make friends and have a good time with kids your own age. You learn how to play together, which is a lot more fun than playing alone.

Teamwork involves sharing and practice. It

means thinking not only of yourself but of what is best for the team. In soccer, as in other sports, each player has a "job" to do. These jobs include defending the goal, moving the ball upfield, and attempting to score. It is fun to be given a job, and then to do it to the best of your ability.

As a member of a soccer team, you have responsibility. Each player must attend practice sessions, listen to the coach, and try to learn as much as possible about the game.

Learning Sportsmanship

Sportsmanship means playing with fairness. Someone who is a good sport plays by the rules, helps other players (even, at times, an opposing player), controls his or her emotions, and is not a "sore loser." Have you ever seen a sporting event on TV in which two players collide, one falls down, and the other helps him up? That's an example of sportsmanship.

Another example comes at the end of a soccer game. After each game, it is proper for the two teams to line up in the middle of the field. They walk toward each other with arms out, giving "high fives," or shaking hands. The two coaches also shake hands. No matter who won, this gesture shows respect for the effort each player made.

Congratulate your teammates as well. Pat them on the back. Tell them they played a good game. You'll be setting an example of good sportsmanship. Your coach will be especially proud of you.

Developing Skills

Soccer is probably the only game you'll ever play in which you're not allowed to use your hands (with the exception of the soccer goalie). You'll be taught how to use your feet to move the ball on the field. At first, that may seem awkward to do.

For each position, there are different skills that are important to learn. A forward needs to use speed to race toward the goal. A fullback must kick strongly to clear the ball to midfield. Most coaches will put players at different positions during a season. In this way, you'll learn how to play every position.

The way to develop skills is to pay attention in practice, follow the coach's instructions, and be alert during a game. Realize that you cannot learn everything at once. For example, being able to pass the ball to a teammate while running is an important skill that may take a while to learn. Be patient.

Getting Healthful Exercise

Soccer is one of the best sports for getting in shape. In soccer, you run up and down the field many times. You constantly use your body going after the ball, avoiding defenders, dribbling, and passing.

Whether you realize it or not, all this activity is very good for you. Doctors know that kids, as well as adults, need exercise to be healthy. The exercise you do in soccer will keep your weight down, give you energy, build up your stamina, and even help you to sleep more soundly.

When you're in shape, and in good health, you

7

feel better, too. Your body will "tell" you if you're not getting enough exercise.

Playing With Rules

Without rules, a soccer game would be a mess. It would be disorganized, unsafe, and no fun. Rules are necessary for your protection, and for your enjoyment of the game. They are enforced by the referee.

Learning the rules, and following them, is a skill in itself. Some rules involve the way you make certain plays. Other rules have to do with the way the game is set up. Once you begin playing, you'll understand why they're important.

Having a Coach

A coach should be a teacher and friend. He or she should help you learn the game and enjoy it. The coach should make you feel proud and treat you with kindness and respect.

Just as you and your teammates have different personalities, so do coaches. Some are strict, others are loose. Some yell a lot, others speak softly. Some are very serious, others kid around.

You may prefer a certain type of coach. However, you might not always have the kind you want. Don't let that bother you. Your coach should always treat you fair and square.

If, for any reason, you feel you are being mistreated, tell your parents. They may help you see that your treatment is not unfair; or, they may decide to discuss your problem with the coach. Parents are

8

supposed to be involved with their kids' teams; they should be able to speak with your coach about how you're doing.

Increasing Self-confidence

Some people shy away from sports like soccer because of fear. They are afraid they won't be good players, or because they don't know anything about the game. Don't be afraid. Everyone begins without knowing the game. As you play and learn, your confidence will grow.

Because soccer is a team sport, all players share in the successes and disappointments. No one player should be "blamed" for a poor team showing, nor cheered for winning a game for the team.

When you gain confidence in your soccer ability, you'll find yourself becoming a more confident person in general. One of the benefits of sports is the feeling that you can always succeed when you put your mind to something.

Pride in the Uniform

It is natural to feel happy when you put on a fresh uniform before a game. Wearing the team colors will give you team spirit. You've earned your uniform— wear it with pride.

When you arrive at a game, your teammates will greet you with excitement. Seeing all your friends in colorful uniforms will get you revved up and raring to play.

Try your best and have fun.

Chapter 2
Soccer Rules

When you play sports with your friends, you make a lot of rules without even realizing it. You decide how many kids will be on each side. You choose which field you'll play on. You decide how long the game will last, and which kind of equipment will be used.

No game can be played without these types of rules. Rules help you understand the game, keep the activity safe, and prevent any player or team from having an unfair advantage.

In soccer, as in other sports, if you don't play by the rules you will be penalized. That will hurt your team. If any player repeatedly breaks the rules, he or she could be forced to leave the game.

In your neighborhood games, you and your friends decide as a group if someone has broken the rules. In soccer, there's a referee who makes those decisions.

A referee may be a teenager with soccer experience or an adult. It could be a man or a woman. In some leagues, a referee is required to wear a black uniform so that he or she is easy to spot on the field. The referee is usually call the "ref," for short. All refs have a whistle that they blow when a rule has been broken. They also have a stopwatch and keep official game time.

Once a referee has made a decision, it stands. Players and coaches are not supposed to argue with the referee. Refs aren't perfect. Every so often, they might make an honest mistake. One time, it might

favor your team; another time, the opposing team. In the end, any mistakes usually even out.

The rules of soccer are sometimes called the "laws of the game." They involve every aspect of the game. The more you know about them, the better player you can become. Here are some of soccer's most important rules:

1. *The field:* A soccer field is in the shape of a rectangle. For professional teams, the length can be

up to 130 yards and the width 100 yards. That's bigger than a football field. For younger age-groups, a typical field might be 100 yards long and 50 yards wide. That's still a lot of ground to cover.

Some fields are smooth, others choppy. Some fields are windy, others are calm. Being aware of the size and type of each field helps coaches and players plan strategy.

2. *The ball:* A soccer ball usually is made of leather as opposed to rubber, and is traditionally white with black lettering and designs. It is a little smaller than a basketball and fairly light, weighing a pound or less. They vary slightly in size and weight. Older players use the bigger balls. There are also plastic balls for young children.

3. *Number of players:* Each team plays 11 players at a time. Most soccer teams have 13 to 15 players in all. From one game to the next, coaches may rotate which players start the game, and which come in as substitutions.

Don't feel bad if you don't start every game. Everyone usually gets to play some part of the game.

4. *Gear:* Because there is body contact in soccer, players are not allowed to wear any type of sharp-edged gear that could harm another player. (There's more information about clothing and equipment in chapter 5.)

5. *Referees:* To repeat: The referee is the boss. In addition to calling penalties, the ref will stop the game when a player appears to be hurt. At that moment, all movement must stop; players sit on the

field and wait. The coach will check the player's condition and, if necessary, take him or her out of the game. Oftentimes, a fallen player is not actually injured, but simply out of breath.   The ref will decide when to resume play.

Soccer is one sport that is played in the rain. If it pours and the ref feels conditions are not safe, he or she may stop the game. In the Olympics, that would never happen. In 1976, 1980, and 1984, the final match of the Olympic soccer tournament was played in a driving rain.

6. *Linesmen:* Usually there are two people, one on each side of the field, who determine which team is out-of-bounds with the ball. They use a flag to signal the referee. Linesmen should not be argued with, either.

7. *Duration of game:* The pros play two 45-minute

halves. Most high school teams play four 20-minute quarters. For ages 12 and under, there are usually two halves of 25 to 30 minutes, with a 10-minute halftime break.

In soccer, the clock runs continuously. Time runs even when the ball goes out-of-bounds or when a goal is scored. It stops only when a player is hurt and the ref halts the game.

8. *Start of play:* A coin toss is used to decide which team kicks off first. One or more players chosen by the coach (frequently the team captains) will meet in the middle of the field with the ref and players from the opposing team. The direction of the wind will affect the decision to kick or defend. After the toss, the players shake hands and both teams take their positions.

9. *Ball in play:* The entire ball must cross the line to be out-of-bounds. If part of the ball is on the line, it's still in play.

10. *Scoring:* Most scoring is done by kicking the ball into the goal. You are also allowed to score by using your head (called "heading") or other parts of your body such as your chest or knee—but not your hands. Each score is worth one point. The team scoring the most goals wins.

11. *Throw-ins:* When the ball goes out-of-bounds past the sideline, a throw-in puts it back in play. A player from the team that did not touch the ball last makes the throw. You must stand behind the line, keep both feet on the ground, and throw the ball with two hands from behind your head. A goal cannot be

scored directly from a throw-in.

12. *Fouls:* You are not allowed to push, trip, hit, hold, or kick an opposing player. If you do, even by accident, the other team will be given a direct free kick from the spot where the misconduct happened. In this case, only the goalie is allowed to defend

against the shot, which makes it easy for the other team to score.

13. *Goal kick:* When the ball goes out-of-bounds past the line near the goal, and is last touched by the team trying to score, the team defending the goal is given a goal kick.

The ball is placed on a marked spot near the goal

and kicked by the defense toward the other end of the field. It must travel 18 feet before a player can touch it.

14. *Corner kick:* In a way, this is the opposite of the goal kick. If a defending player last touches a ball that goes over the line near the goal, a corner kick is given to the team trying to score.

The ball is placed on the corner of the field, and the team's best kicker is given a chance to score from that angle.

15. *Age:* Teams in community leagues are almost always based on age. There are teams for 8-year-olds, 9-year-olds, and so on. Kids are usually grouped according to the year in which they were born. For example: the '81s, or the '82s. Teams of the same age play against one another. Sometimes, in a practice game, a young team that is very good will go against older players.

16. *Ties:* Tie scores usually are left that way; there's no overtime period in soccer. However, an exception may be made in tournament finals.

To break a tie, a "shootout" will be held. The ball is placed a short distance from the goal and each player is given one turn at a free kick. The goalie tries to prevent a score. The team that scores the most goals wins.

17. *Sportsmanship:* Any player using foul or abusive language, or continually pushing or elbowing, can be ordered off the field. Coaches can also be scolded or thrown out of a game for cursing or criticizing the ref. Everyone has to keep his or her emotions under control.

Chapter 3

Soccer Skills

Soccer is easy to learn. You just have to use your head (in more ways that one, as you will find out). But first you must learn to use your feet. In most sports, you play with your hands. In soccer, you work the ball with your feet.

In learning soccer skills, you must follow directions, be alert, and pay attention to your coach. Be aware of other players and how they learn. Realize that you cannot learn everything at once.

There are eight soccer skills to concentrate on. They are: 1) dribbling, 2) passing, 3) kicking, 4) shooting, 5) trapping, 6) heading, 7) tackling, and 8) the throw-in.

Dribbling

Dribbling means moving the ball. You tap it or push it, trying to keep control of the ball. Usually a player on the opposing team will be trying to take it away from you.

You can dribble in any direction, and with either foot. Young players should look at the ball as little as possible when they dribble. With experience, you'll be able to look up all the time, giving you a better view of other players.

Dribble with the sides of your foot, not the toe.

17

Keep the ball on the inside of your foot when taking short steps in a small area. When running down the field, use the outside of your foot on the ball.

As you dribble, keep your knees bent and body positioned over the ball. Don't make the mistake of dribbling the ball too far in front of you.

To improve dribbling, practice it a lot. Run down a field or any open space with the ball. Do it slowly at first, then build speed. Take a few steps, then go farther.

Don't just dribble in one direction. Move the ball to your left and right. Turn around and dribble in the opposite direction.

Set up balls or cones as obstacles and dribble around them. You can even try to fake one way and dribble the other way. Make believe the obstacle is another player.

Passing

Young players usually dribble too much. "Get rid of the ball," coaches call out. The more any one player dribbles, the better chance the opposing players have to steal the ball.

As in dribbling, use the sides of your feet to pass

the ball. Look for a teammate nearby, and push the ball sharply toward him or her. This is called a "push" pass.

Make sure your foot does not wobble when you make contact with the ball. Keep it steady. That way your pass will be strong and accurate.

While keeping your eyes on the ball, also take a peek at your teammate. Pass the ball low, aiming for your teammate's feet.

Practice passing with friends and teammates. A good pass that sets up a goal is just as important as the shot that scores the goal.

Kicking

Dribbling is a form of kicking. Shooting is, too. Kicking is done to send the ball far down the field,

and also after various penalties are called.

Kicking for height and distance is different from making a short pass. Try to step into the ball, as a field goal kicker does in football. Swing your kicking foot behind you and follow through with your foot after making contact. Look right at the ball, not at where it's going. After the kick, your foot should be high in the air.

Shooting

There are many ways to shoot the ball. A player could be alone, racing toward the goal. This is called a "breakaway." In this case, only the goalie would defend against the shot.

Even if you have a clear shot, don't assume it will be an easy one. Too many players think scoring a goal is a breeze. Then, they miss the shot.

Shoot the ball low. If it's high in the air, the goalie has a better chance of blocking it. Dribble to within a few feet of the goal, then shoot. A long shot is easier for the goalie to snag.

Kick with the side of your foot. Put a lot of weight into the shot. Aim carefully, think fast, and pay close attention to where the goalie is positioned.

When opposing players are close to you, your shot will be more difficult. Use your best dribbling to maneuver away from the defenders. Then take the shot.

Practice shooting into an open net with a teammate playing goalie. Backyard goals can be purchased in sporting goods stores. Even though they're small, they're very useful.

A good scorer should be versatile. That means he or she can score from many angles. Practice kicking into every part of the goal, and from different points on the field.

Trapping

Trapping in soccer means catching the ball. When the ball is in the air and coming toward you,

you must "catch" or stop it, by allowing the ball to hit a part of your body (other than your hands). Use your

21

chest, legs, or feet. This is also called "collecting" the ball.

Follow the ball in the air and position your body so you can trap it. Be aware of other players so you know what to do with the ball when you receive it. Will you dribble, or pass?

To trap the ball with your chest, keep your legs apart and bend your knees. Lean backward so the ball falls on your chest and drops in front of you. Don't be afraid of the ball or close your eyes; don't tense up.

If you stiffen up, the ball will bounce off you and go to another player. Relax; be confident. Your body should be like a cushion for the ball.

Heading

Heading is a difficult play. Hitting the ball off your head just to show that you can do it has no purpose. Always ask yourself this: How can I best

control the ball?

In heading, use your forehead. Before trying it in a game, do it softly in practice many times. Bounce the ball off your head. See how it feels.

To head the ball with power, you'll have to jump into it. Don't worry much about heading, though; it's the least important skill for beginning players.

Tackling

Tackling (also called charging) is a way to take the ball from your opponent. It's a defensive move, to be done by any player. All soccer players must learn to play offense and defense.

In tackling, you charge the player who has the ball. Use your feet, legs, and body to disrupt his or her movement and spring the ball loose so you can get it.

You are not allowed to use your hands or elbows. You cannot push or grab another player. Lean into a player with your shoulder to get the ball. When the ball is loose, either pass it or keep it yourself.

Good tackling forces the dribbler to make a bad pass, kick the ball out-of-bounds or simply lose the ball. You must be aggressive. Usually you end up "fighting" for the ball. Don't give up.

The Throw-in

The throw-in is harder than it looks. In sports like baseball and football, you use one hand to throw a ball. In soccer, you must keep both hands on the ball and both feet on the ground. If you don't, the ref will give the ball to the other team.

Hold the ball on both sides and fling it out. Don't let one hand do most of the work. Make sure both hands push the ball firmly.

Many young players don't bother to aim their throw-ins. If you just throw the ball anywhere, the other team usually ends up with it. Aim for a teammate, or for an open spot your teammate can run to. Think before you throw.

Chapter 4

Soccer Teamwork

The players on a soccer team must work together. If they don't, the team won't play as well or have as much fun.

There are eleven positions on a soccer field. The coach gives each player a position. With two teams on the field at once, there are 22 players in action.

The smartest thing you can do in soccer is play your position. That means moving around only in your area. It does not mean running all over the field after the ball.

At almost every game, you'll hear coaches shout: "Play your position! Play your position!"

In practice, the coach shows you where to stand on the field and what to do when the ball comes toward you. During a game, however, many players get excited. They forget what they learned in practice. They make the mistake of leaving their positions to follow the ball.

The best way to score a goal is by passing the ball around. Eventually, someone will get off a good shot. If everyone crowds around the ball, there won't be anyone to pass to. No matter where the ball goes, play your position!

In soccer, there is a goalie plus ten other positions. The other positions usually are set up in three

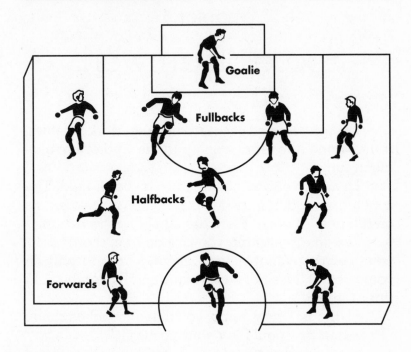

Goalie

Fullbacks

Halfbacks

Forwards

rows. These rows are spaced out so they can work together.

Forwards play in the front row. There are three forwards. The player in the middle is called the center forward. The other two are called wings—left wing and right wing.

The middle row players are called halfbacks, or midfielders. There are three of them, too: left, center, and right.

The back row is made up of fullbacks, who are also called defenders. There are four of them: one on the left, one on the right, and two in the center. Sometimes, one of the center fullbacks is placed a little farther back and called a "sweeper."

The sweeper, a strong player, is given extra space in which to move and assist other players in defending the goal.

You'll find that a coach will use different strategies in the way he or she positions the players, but you should know what each player is supposed to do, and how they all work together.

Goalie

The job of the goalie is to prevent the other team from scoring. The goalie stands in front of the goal. When a shot is made, the goalie tries to stop the ball by catching or hitting it away.

A goalie needs to have "good hands." Once a shot is made, you have to move your hands quickly; you need good reflexes. Like other skills, this comes with practice.

Keep your eyes on the ball at all times. If players are bunched together, the ball may be difficult to see. Concentrate, be alert, and think about where the ball will go next.

Where will you stand at the goal? Will you be in the middle, or on the left or right side? A smart goalie stands directly between the goal and the person with the ball. This is known as "cutting the angle." You give the shooter as little clear space as possible to aim at.

When you stop a shot, it's called a save. If you

stop a shot but don't catch the ball, quickly pick up the ball so the shooter doesn't get a second shot.

Once you have the ball, you must get it back to your teammates. You do this by throwing, rolling, or kicking it. The kick used is a punt, just like in football.

Look for a teammate who is open. Don't just punt the ball in any direction without thinking.

Sometimes goalies have to jump for the ball, or even dive for it. Think of the goal area as your home. You must do all you can to protect it.

Forwards

Forwards are the main scorers on the team. They are good dribblers who must learn to pass the ball accurately on the run. If they play their positions—left, center, and right—they have the best chance to make good passes.

Forwards must be unselfish players. It does not matter who scores. Some forwards are better at helping other forwards to score than at scoring themselves.

Coaches like to put a lefty at left wing. From the left side of the field, a lefty has a better angle on the goal than a right-footed kicker does.

Forwards do a lot of fast running. They need to work on their speed and also have the endurance to last an entire game.

Halfbacks

Halfback may be the hardest position in soccer. Because you're in the middle of the field, you must play hard on both offense and defense. You're always on the move.

On defense, you must stop an attack. Challenge your opponents; be aggressive. Go for the ball.

Always think about how the ball will travel, and how other players will move. Try to beat your opponent to the ball. Use your best trapping skills.

On offense, your job is to get the ball to the forwards. Learn how your forwards move so you can pass with accuracy. Make your passes quick and strong.

Don't do a lot of dribbling. If you can't pass to a forward, pass to another halfback. Keep the ball low for the best control.

29

After you move the ball up to the forwards, keep your eyes on the ball and be ready to switch to defense. The opposing team could steal the ball, and you'll have to be ready for that.

Fullbacks

Fullbacks should be very good kickers. When the ball is close to their goal, they have to kick it hard toward midfield. Soft kicks will only keep the ball within scoring distance.

As defenders, fullbacks guard the opposing team's forwards. Fullbacks must be fast and aggressive.

Guard the forwards closely. Don't give them room to dribble or maneuver. Position yourself between the forward and the goal.

Try to force the forward to the outside of the field, away from the goal. From that point, a shot would be very hard. Also, you can then kick the ball out-of-bounds, forcing a throw-in.

If the forward you're guarding is extremely fast, you may have to allow your opponent some room. Otherwise, he or she could dart around you and be free for a shot. Learn to judge how best to play each opponent.

Whether you're a forward, halfback, or fullback, the most important lesson you can learn is: Play your position.

Chapter 5

Soccer Gear

Part of the excitement of soccer is having the right clothing and equipment. It makes you feel like you're learning the game. Also, with the right gear, you'll feel comfortable and protect yourself against injury.

Soccer equipment is available at most sporting goods stores and department stores. You don't need very much to get started.

Soccer ball: Balls vary slightly in weight and size. Each type has a different number, such as number 3 or number 4. The younger the player, the lighter and smaller the ball. You should buy a ball that fits your age. Players of ages 8 to 12 would probably use a number 4 ball.

If you're on a team, the coach may ask you to bring your own ball to practices. Since most balls look alike, write your name on your ball so you take home the right one.

Soccer shoes: At first, it's fine to play soccer in your regular, everyday sneakers. But make sure the sneakers are sturdy. If they're worn out, you could end up hurting your foot.

As you improve your play, you'll need to purchase shoes made for soccer. These are called cleats. They are usually black, and made of leather. On the bottom they have thick nubs that give you traction when you run.

Since soccer is played on grass, good traction is important. Games are played in the rain, on wet fields. If you wear sneakers, you may slip and fall.

If you buy cleats, use them only for soccer. You'll ruin your cleats if you walk around in them, or use them for other sports played on concrete surfaces.

After a game, your cleats will be dirty and may

be caked in mud. Clean your cleats and keep them dry. Make sure they're clean on the inside, too.

A good pair of cleats can make you a better player. They help you move on the field, and also make your foot "stronger." With cleats, you'll gain better control of the ball. You'll have a more solid kick.

Soccer shirt: A soccer shirt is also called a jersey. As with shoes, you don't need an official shirt at first. Any T-shirt or sweatshirt will do.

Many teams will give you uniforms or ask you to buy a certain style or color of shirt. There are many types of soccer jerseys. Usually, one is enough, as long as it's kept clean.

Make sure you buy a short-sleeved jersey. If you play in the cold, you can always put a long-sleeved shirt under your soccer jersey. When it's very cold, some players wear gloves and hats.

Soccer shorts: Don't play in a pair of cutoff shorts. Those are not made for sports. You need shorts for athletic use, which are light and roomy.

Shorts that people use for jogging are good. If you receive a team uniform, you may find the shorts come down low on your leg, almost to your knees. Make sure your shorts are comfortable and don't annoy you when you run. Tuck your shirt into your shorts.

Many people today wear leggings, or tights, in sports because they feel snug and keep you warm. Don't wear them in soccer unless it's very cold. In chilly weather, remember to bring heavy clothing to wear over your soccer clothing before a game, and when you're on the sidelines.

Soccer socks: Most players wear high socks that come up near the knee. Make sure there's elastic at the top of the socks so they won't roll down. You should own at least three pair of socks for soccer. If it's raining, take an extra pair to a game.

Shin guards: In soccer, you'll likely get kicked in the shins a lot. It's part of the game. Shin guards protect your shins. Socks can be worn underneath or over your shin guards.

Water bottle: To feel refreshed, always take a plastic water bottle to practices and games. Fill it with cold water and ice or a sports drink. This is absolutely necessary in warm weather, but a good idea even when it's cool. In soccer, running around builds up a keen thirst. If you don't drink after sweating, you can get sick.

Goalies: Soccer rules require the goalie to wear a different-colored shirt than the other players. Players often switch off playing goalie; there may be three or four different goalies in one game. You simply share a large shirt, which is worn over your uniform.

Safety rules: All jewelry must be removed before a game. That includes watches, rings, earrings, and necklaces. Eyeglasses can be worn, and can be safely secured with a band that straps around your head. Playing with any sharp object on your body or clothes can hurt other people, or cause yourself harm.

Chapter 6

Soccer Conditioning

Soccer is a nonstop game in which players move continuously without a break. Other than half-time, there's no letup. This puts extra stress on the body, and having good skills won't be enough to get you through the game.

A player might run as much as two or three miles in a single game. To really enjoy soccer, you should be physically fit. Otherwise, you'll hear coaches shouting from the sidelines: "You're getting beat to the ball!"

Even the best athletes need to work at being in shape. That's why professional leagues have training camps prior to the regular season. All ball players need to limber up, work their muscles, and perhaps even lose some weight in order to throw, catch, pass, run, kick—do whatever is needed in their particular sport.

Have you ever gotten out of breath while playing sports? Have you ever run down a field and felt your body grow weak, your leg muscles tighten, and your lungs feel ready to burst? Athletes young and old experience these feelings at one time or another. They are part of the process of getting in shape.

As you condition yourself, you improve your physical fitness. Your muscles become stronger. Your joints become looser. You'll breath easier when you run hard. You'll gain speed, too, which is very important in soccer.

Fitness takes time. It can't happen in one day or one week. Be patient. Don't overdo it. Making progress at a gradual pace brings the best results.

By getting in shape, you'll reduce risk of injury. Soccer is a contact sport, and players often collide. You dive for the ball, change directions quickly, and play on muddy fields. A well-conditioned player will be less likely to get hurt.

If you're just learning the game, conditioning can help you make up for weaknesses. "If you can hustle, you'll outplay your opponents," advises Joe Santos, a former professional player who directs the soccer program at Kutsher's Sports Academy in Monticello, New York.

"For young players," Santos emphasizes, "the most important thing is being able to run the field without getting tired."

Santos and other coaches instruct players to get in shape while using the soccer ball. That way, you can develop your skills at the same time.

For example, Santos will have his players dribble the ball. When he blows a whistle, they have to run fast while continuing to dribble. This not only develops your speed but also the ability to control the ball as you would during a "breakaway" in a game.

Another good dribbling drill is one in which three players are spread out on a field. They move the ball down the field, passing to each other while running at top speed.

For a running activity without the ball, a group of players can line up one in front of the other. The group runs in a line down the field. They start slowly, build speed, and finish fast. Each time the run is repeated, a player moves from the back of the line to the front.

The fast running in soccer puts a lot of pressure on the upper front leg muscles, called the quadriceps. When you run fast, you lift your knees high; the "quads" support the knee and fatigue quickly if they're not strong.

To strengthen the quadriceps, try hopping back and forth over a short bench. Do this for 20 seconds, then rest. Then hop for 30 seconds, rest; hop for 45 seconds, then a minute. If a bench seems too high, simply hop over a soccer ball.

As you work the legs, you may find your stomach is weak. Experienced athletes have learned that each part of the body affects another part. A soft belly will slow you down. Sit-ups will strengthen your stomach, though. Try to do 25 to 50 almost every day. Do them slowly, keeping your knees bent.

One of the best soccer players in America, John Harkes, does 200 sit-ups every day, plus many other forms of exercise, to stay in tiptop shape. Harkes, named the number-one high school player in the U.S. in 1984, is a member of the U.S. National Team that plays against teams from other countries.

If you get tired during a game, you won't be able to use your skills to their utmost. Imagine trying to pass or shoot when your legs are caving in. Or think of fighting for the ball when you feel like you need a nap.

Remember that almost any open space, including your backyard, can be used to work on soccer conditioning. And you don't need a whole team, either. Practice with a couple of friends, or even on your own.

The more your physical fitness improves, the less you'll experience the most frustrating feeling of all in soccer: getting beat to the ball.

Chapter 7

Soccer Organization and Stars

The modern game of soccer began in England in the middle 1800s. It was called football—after all, you use your feet—and still goes by that name in England and other countries outside the United States. In Spain, soccer is called *futbol;* in Brazil, *futebol;* in Holland, *voetbal.*

Naturally, in the U.S. the game cannot be called "football." We have another major sport called football, while other countries do not.

A form of soccer can be traced to China as far back as 1697 B.C. The ancient Greeks and Romans also played a type of soccer. Soccer is now played in more than 150 countries—almost every nation on earth.

Soccer became popular in the U.S. in the early 1900s. In 1913, the United States Soccer Federation (USSF) was formed. This organization oversees all levels of the sport, from youth leagues to professional teams. It is also a member of the worldwide organizing body, known as the International Federation of Association Football, or FIFA.

According to the USSF, there are more than 5 million youth soccer players (19 and under) in the U.S.

The sport is growing in all parts of the country. These are the different branches of the sport:

World Cup

The World Cup is the world championship of soccer. It was first held in 1930 and is conducted once every four years. Italy and Brazil, two countries where soccer is the major sport, have won the World Cup three times each. The U.S. has never won it.

The World Cup tournament is held in a different country each time. The games receive as much attention as a World Series or Super Bowl. In 1994, it will be staged in the U.S. for the first time.

Professional Leagues

In 1977, the North American Soccer League drew a record crowd of over 77,000 fans to a game at Giants Stadium in New Jersey. Sports followers thought soccer had finally reached the bigtime in the U.S. But interest in the soccer professionals gradually faded, and the NASL folded in 1985.

Spurred by the enthusiasm of 1977, that same year the Major Indoor Soccer League (MISL) was formed. The league has continued to this day, and currently has seven teams. An indoor field is smaller than those outdoors. The MISL arena is about 200 feet long by 85 feet wide.

Compared to other pro athletes, soccer players in the U.S. make very little money. In other countries, however, soccer stars receive large salaries.

40

Professional leagues in Europe and South America draw crowds of over 100,000 spectators. These fans get so excited that fights sometimes break out. People have been hurt, and even killed, by violent mobs.

Olympic Games

Because the World Cup is so important, an Olympic title is not the number-one goal, as in many other sports. In fact, players who have competed in the World Cup are ineligible for the Olympics.

The U.S. has never won an Olympic soccer tournament. The best American finish was in 1900, when teams from the U.S. placed second and third. There is no women's soccer in the Olympics or World Cup. The 1992 Summer Olympics will be held in Barcelona, Spain.

College Soccer

Almost all colleges have soccer teams for men and women. The National Collegiate Athletic Association (NCAA), as well as other college groups, hold championships in soccer every year.

The team with the best record in college soccer has been the University of North Carolina women's team. In 1988, UNC won its sixth NCAA title in seven years and extended its winning streak to 70 games.

Other colleges with excellent soccer programs include the University of Virginia, Santa Clara, North Carolina State, Connecticut, Clemson, Indiana, and

Hartwick. At many colleges, there are also "intramural" programs—where players compete against teams from their own school.

High School

There are boys' and girls' soccer teams in virtually every high school. Soccer is usually a fall sport. Many colleges offer scholarships to outstanding high school players.

Youth Soccer

Almost every city, town, or community in the U.S. has a recreational soccer league. Kids as young as 5 or 6 can join. Games may be played in both fall and spring; in some cases, indoor games may be held during the winter.

Many of these leagues have all-star teams known as "traveling teams." These teams play all-star squads from other communities. Sometimes, they travel to tournaments held in other states.

Many youth leagues are part of the United States Youth Soccer Federation. This group promotes soccer by reviewing new rules, teaching coaches, holding tournaments, and selecting top players to be members of national youth teams.

Adult Clubs

Many cities have soccer clubs for adults who might play once every week or two for fun, and to stay in good shape.

42

Soccer's Greatest Stars

Pelé

The one soccer player known throughout the United States and the world is the Brazilian known as Pelé. He is considered the game's all-time greatest and most exciting player. Pelé (pronounced pay-LAY) retired in 1977, after a 22-year career.

Pelé was beloved by millions of fans, and respected by his competitors. His love of soccer and his amazing feats on the field packed stadiums worldwide. As a superstar, he was also very modest.

Pelé was born in 1940 in a village of 170 people. The eldest of three children, he was named Edson Arantes do Nascimento. By age 7 or 8, he was given the nickname "Pelé." He does not remember why.

He began playing soccer barefoot. Pelé became a teenage sensation (wearing soccer shoes), and at age 17 he was the youngest member of the Brazilian team in the 1958 World Cup. Brazil won the championship game that year and again in 1962 and 1970.

Pelé's professional team in Brazil was called Santos. He played 18 years with Santos, scoring 1,220 goals in 1,253 games. That's a record that may never be equaled.

In 1975, Pelé came to the U.S. to play for the Cosmos team of the North American Soccer League. Pelé was an instant hero in the U.S. He played his final game for the Cosmos in 1977 and has since returned to his native Brazil.

43

Kyle Rote, Jr.

Kyle Rote, Jr., who played football, basketball, and baseball in high school, took up soccer in college and went on to star in the NASL.

The son of former pro football star Kyle Rote, he is one of the few American-born players to earn soccer stardom. His biggest success, however, came in TV's "Superstars" event, which is a competition among many champions involving several different sports. In 1974, Rote won the event, defeating the likes of Reggie Jackson (baseball) and O.J. Simpson (football).

Franz Beckenbauer

Franz Beckenbauer, from West Germany, led his nation to victory in the 1974 World Cup. In 1977, he came to the U.S. to join the Cosmos of the NASL. He became a teammate of Pelé's.

In 1978, a special day was held in his honor, and over 70,000 fans turned out to pay him tribute.

Giorgio Chinaglia

Another player who starred for the Cosmos, Giorgio Chinaglia came to the U.S. from Italy in 1976. In Italy, he was the number-one scorer on his club, leading it to the Italian league championship. Chinaglia was the highest paid player in all of Italy. When he left Italy for the U.S., he enraged Italian soccer fans.

Chinaglia found America to his liking and has done much to help young players develop.

44

Shep Messing

Shep Messing proved that excellence in the classroom could go together with being a soccer star. Messing attended Harvard University, where he was a top student. He was also an All-America goalie who was selected to the 1972 Olympic soccer team. He set an Olympic record for saves.

Steve Zungul

Steve Zungul is a Yugoslavian who has starred in the U.S. in the Major Indoor Soccer League. He is the league's all-time scoring leader, and was voted Player of the Decade in 1988. He holds or shares 40 MISL scoring records and currently plays for the Tacoma Stars of Tacoma, Washington.

Diego Maradona

Diego Maradona of Argentina is currently the leading superstar in all of soccer. He plays for a team in Naples, Italy, and earns over $1 million a year in salary and product endorsements.

Maradona, 29, grew up in Buenos Aires, Argentina, and began to play soccer professionally at the age of 15. He is treated like a movie star in Argentina. Maradona's marriage in Buenos Aires in 1989 was considered the biggest event of the year. Over 1,000 people attended the wedding reception.

Todd Haskins

At 16 years of age, Todd Haskins of Columbia, Maryland, is a future international star. A top high school and club player, he already has international experience.

As a member of the U.S. 16-and-under team in 1988 and 1989, Haskins has played championship games in Scotland, Israel, and in other countries. Some day, perhaps, he will be as outstanding as Pelé.

Chapter 8

Training Rules

When it comes to staying in shape, the first rule of sports is: Use it or lose it.

That means, any part of your body that you don't put to use regularly becomes weak. This includes your arms, legs, shoulders, stomach—even your mind.

If you ride your bicycle almost every day, you'll be able to travel a good distance without getting tired. If you stop riding for a few weeks, you'll find that when you start up again, it may be a struggle to go very far. You may have trouble making it up a hill that used to feel easy.

"Use it or lose it." Sooner or later, every young athlete realizes how important that rule is. There are many other rules on building your body for sports, staying in shape, and preventing injury. Being aware of them will help you in soccer and other sports as well.

1. *Stay in shape:* Try to do some form of exercise at least three times a week. It does not matter whether you do it by yourself or as part of a team.

2. *Have fun:* Pick sports that you enjoy so that you look forward to doing them.

3. *Plan ahead:* Contact friends in advance to

organize sports activities.

4. *Be flexible:* At times, you may have to play a sport someone else has chosen. That's okay. Next time, you'll get to choose the activity.

5. *Variety is best:* Experiment with different sports. Even if soccer is your favorite, try something else, too, so you don't get bored.

Many adults who exercise now vary their activities. One day they run; the next day they might swim or bike. This is known as "cross-training."

If you're on a soccer team but also swim or play basketball, that's cross-training, too. Cross-training is an excellent way to keep your body in the best possible shape.

6. *Dress properly:* In the cold, wear an extra jersey, sweatshirt, or jacket. Have a hat and gloves ready. It's better to have more clothing than you need, than not enough.

In the heat, wear loose-fitting clothing. Light colors are cooler than dark because they don't absorb the heat.

7. *Eat properly:* Diet is important in giving you the fuel for exercise. What you eat can affect how you feel before a game. For more on good and bad foods, see chapter 9.

8. *Get enough rest:* Kids your age, especially those involved in sports, need at least eight hours of sleep a night. If you have difficulty sleeping, make sure you tell your parents.

Rest involves more than sleep, though; it also means taking a break from hard exercise. It's a health hazard to play hard day in and day out. Even the pros have occasional days off.

9. *Be patient:* Getting in shape is a gradual process. It's a kind of learning for your body. Just like you can't become a whiz at math overnight, you can't develop your body in a short time, either.

10. *Be specific:* Your body gets in shape in specific ways. Running, for example, strengthens your legs. Swimming strengthens your arms.

Not all running is the same either. For soccer, fast running is better than slow running, because your movement on the field, is in short, fast bursts.

During the soccer season, when you're practicing, and playing games regularly, you probably don't need to do a lot of extra exercise. When you're not playing, try to run or bicycle a couple of times a week, and also swim and do some stretching exercises.

11. *Warm up:* Before play, always warm up by jogging, stretching, and kicking the ball around. This will loosen you up. Coaches usually have players warm up together.

12. *Cool down:* After playing, everyone usually rushes away. If necessary, "cool down" on your own with more stretching. Your muscles will thank you for this the next day.

13. *Drink plenty of fluids:* Always take a water bottle to practices and games. Drink before the game, during halftime, and after the game. You sweat in the cold as well as the heat, so you must drink even when it's cold out.

A smart coach will allow you to drink as much as

you want. There are some coaches who may disallow players from drinking as a form of punishment for not following instructions. This is wrong. If that happens to you, tell your parents, who may need to discuss this with the coach. Not drinking when you need to can make you sick. If a coach is foolish, you must alert your parents or another coach or school official.

14. *Girls and boys:* Training benefits both girls and boys, in virtually the same ways. There should be no differences in how boys and girls exercise, learn soccer, practice, or play games.

Chapter 9

Good Food

Did you know that many of the foods that you love to eat are really very good for you as a young soccer player? Does your mouth water at the thought of a pizza pie? Do you get hungry when someone mentions roast turkey? Your answer probably is, "You bet!"

Pizza and turkey are two kinds of meals that are not only enjoyable, they are also "healthy." Foods that are good for you don't have to taste bad.

You've probably heard the phrase "balanced diet." Milk, bread, meat, fish, fruits, and vegetables are some foods that go into a balanced diet. Imagine how you'd feel if you ate only one kind of food. Pretty awful, right?

Many people assume foods like pizza and turkey are not healthy to eat. That is because they put toppings like sausage on their pizza. And they smother their turkey with a heavy gravy.

Plain pizza usually is made of cheese, tomato sauce, and dough. There's nothing unhealthy about that. If you put vegetables like pepper or mushroom on your pizza, that's okay, too. However, sausage and pepperoni have a lot of fat in them.

Fat in foods slows you down and clogs your system. It makes you feel weak and tired. It's like putting sand instead of gas in your car's engine. The car won't be able to move.

As an athlete, you have to zip around like a sports car. Your body is like an engine: It needs fuel. Fat is an example of the wrong fuel.

Fat is found in large amounts of "fast" foods. The meals that you eat at roadside burger restaurants are high in fats.

The first rule of eating for sports is: *Eat as little fat as possible*. It'll only make you heavy. And you won't feel right.

The second rule of eating for sports is: *Plan ahead*.

If you don't plan ahead, you could wind up with a side pain during a soccer game. You've probably felt this type of pain during sports.

It's known as a "stitch." Eating too close to a game can cause this to happen to you. So can eating fatty foods that are not easily digested and used for energy. If you eat burgers and fries right before a game, you may feel like a "blob."

Top athletes know this and try their best to eat to win. They make sure they know when practices and games are scheduled. Eating at least two hours before exercise is a good plan.

During the week, when you attend school, your sports activities are held late in the afternoon. When this happens, your breakfast and lunch are most important. On weekends, when play often is in the morning, your dinner the night before and breakfast that day—if you have one—become crucial.

Should you eat the morning of a game? Only if

you finish eating at least two hours before play. Get up early. Have a light breakfast, such as cereal with skim milk and a banana, muffins, fruit, or yogurt. Make sure you drink, too—water, juice, or milk.

Some people have trouble digesting milk products. If you're one of them, be very careful. Also, stay away from that favorite American breakfast: bacon and eggs. Meat and eggs are high in fat.

For sports, just about the best food you can eat is probably one of your favorites: spaghetti. Spaghetti, lasagna, ziti, and other noodle dishes are all types of pasta.

Pasta is high-performance fuel for the human engine. It contains almost no fat but plenty of carbohydrates. Your muscles love carbohydrates. They devour them for fuel.

Some people think spaghetti is a fattening food. It is if you drown it in fatty toppings. Tomato sauce is best. Go easy on the meatballs and sausage.

As you can tell, the third rule of eating for sports

53

is: *When in doubt, stick with pasta.*

School lunches, eaten close to sports activity, must be handled with care. One recent survey reported that the average school lunch is 39 percent fat. That's much too high.

If you bring lunch from home, pack a sandwich of chicken, turkey, or cheese. Have some fruit. Drink juice, not soda pop. If you buy lunch, choose soup, salad, or a light sandwich; nothing too spicy like a hot dog, hoagie, or a bowl of chili.

Don't fall for the myth that a candy bar provides a boost of energy. Sweets may trigger a "sugar high," but it's like riding a roller coaster: First you feel up, then down.

So far you've seen that many different types of foods are good for you, and good-tasting, too. This leads to the fourth rule: *Eat a variety of foods.*

No food is totally "bad" as long as you don't make a habit of it. Candy, cake, ice cream? They're okay once in a while. Even Big Macs and Whoppers are all right—maybe once a week, not as an everyday meal.

If you're like a lot of kids, you may have parents who work very hard. They may not have much time to prepare meals at home, or even to shop for food. They're always in a hurry.

Why don't you help out? Learn to make some meals on your own. It's fun, and your parents will appreciate it.

The final rule is: *Preparing your own meals is a healthy habit.* Start with spaghetti and work your way up to a homemade pizza.

Chapter 10

Setting Goals

Goals are a big part of sports. Whenever you watch a sports event on TV, you see sports reporters asking top athletes, "What are your goals for this season?" Whether it's Orel Hershiser, Michael Jordan, or Wayne Gretzky, each athlete always has specific goals in mind.

At the professional level, the goal might be to lead a team to the championship, break a record, or make a comeback following an injury. Pros do not always like to reveal their goals. Some feel it could help other teams make plans to beat them.

The most important goal for the United States National Soccer Team is to make it into the finals of the World Cup, which is held every four years. The World Cup is the World Series of soccer. Of the 113 countries that field national teams, only 24 qualify for the World Cup tournament. In 1990, the U.S. earned a berth in the finals for the first time in 40 years.

A goal, whether connected to professional leagues or neighborhood teams, is something you'd like to achieve. You probably have goals all the time and do not realize it. They may involve friends, family, school, or hobbies. When you study for a test or save money to buy a friend a birthday present, you certainly have goals in mind. Goals can help you achieve in all aspects of life.

Some goals are short-term and may be a few weeks or months away. Others are long-term and may be months or even years into the future. It's good to have both kinds of goals. A goal that's coming up may help you improve your sports play soon. A goal that's long off will encourage you to stick with your plan, and achieve other goals along the way.

Why You Need Goals

A goal requires a plan. You cannot go from point A to point B unless you first decide how to get there. Goals force you to map out a plan, and then follow it. Goals also help you to see your strengths and weaknesses—what you do best, and where you need extra work.

If you play sports with goals, you'll gain an advantage. In soccer, one of the first skills you'll learn will be dribbling. Suppose you're a righty; dribbling the ball with your left foot won't be so easy. If you give yourself the goal of dribbling well with both feet, and practice with your "weak" foot, it will become stronger. Step by step, you'll see improvement. Eventually you'll reach your goal.

Determining Your Goals

Success in sports is almost guaranteed as long as you keep your goals realistic. If you're put at forward, a scoring position in soccer, don't say, "I'm going to be the team's best scorer." Tell yourself: "I'm going to learn how to shoot the best I can."

Take your goal and break it down into small parts. In shooting, you have to set up your shot, position your foot, be aware of other players, and try to outsmart the goalie. A sensible goal to begin with would be to learn how to kick the ball so it travels with speed toward the soccer goal. Don't try for everything at once.

Your goals must be logical for your age, experience, ability, and the time you have to put into a sport. You also have to consider whether certain equipment or facilities are available to you, if you have a coach to work with—even weather conditions.

Choose short-term goals that are realistic, and encourage you to progress from week to week. Choose long-term goals that keep you motivated, and don't make impossible demands on yourself.

Achieving Your Goals

Marathon runner Bill Rodgers could tell you every run he's taken in the last ten years. All he'd have to do is look it up.

Like many top athletes, Rodgers keeps a log, or diary, of his sports development. It includes how long he runs, how fast, and how he felt. He checks it every so often to see what strategy works best for him.

You should do this, too. Take an ordinary notebook and make it into a soccer log. Set it up like a calendar, and write down the details of practices and games so you'll be able to keep track of your progress.

For a practice, take note of the skills you worked on, and how you feel you're doing. For a game, put down the team you played, who won, and the score. Also include which positions you played, how you handled the ball, and whether the coach seemed pleased with the team effort. You can also write down anything funny or unusual that may have happened.

Think of your goal as a "result" and your efforts to achieve it as an "action." The two must go together: action and result. Ask yourself, "What action must I take to achieve what I want?" If the result you want is not to feel tired toward the end of a game, your action should be to get into better shape.

Many young players who wish to improve at soccer decide that the "action" to take is to attend a soccer camp during the summer. These camps usually run for a week or two. They are organized by coaches and are open to anyone. If you'd like to attend a camp, ask your coach for information about it.

Direct your goals toward yourself. If you focus on beating or outplaying someone, you may become frustrated, since you can't control another person's efforts. Work on what *you* can do to improve.

Don't be bashful about asking for help. Parents, teachers, coaches, teammates, and sports doctors can be called on for advice, pointers, and encouragement. Others with more knowledge can make a difference to you as a young athlete.

Be patient. Never lose sight of your goals.

Glossary

Soccer Talk

You've learned a lot of new words, names, and phrases that are part of the language of soccer. Here's a summary of key terms, in alphabetical order. Try to know them all.

breakaway: when an attacking player breaks away from the defense, and is alone near the goal with a chance to score

charging: using your body to push an opposing player and get control of the ball (also known as tackling)

cleats: hard shoes with grooves on the bottom to give you traction on soft fields

cool-down: easy exercise to relax your body after a practice or game

cross-training: using different sports to get into the best possible shape

dribbling: controling the ball with your feet

football: what soccer is called in most countries outside the United States

forward: player who takes shots, and scores goals

foul: when you break the rules by playing roughly, resulting in a penalty kick

free kick: a kick at the goal awarded to a team

when the other team is penalized

fullback: defensive player who tries to prevent the other team from scoring

goalie: player who guards the goal and tries to block shots (only player allowed to use hands)

halfback: midfield player who covers both offense and defense

heading: using your head to trap or move the ball

juggling: a practice drill in which you use your

feet or legs to keep the ball in the air

linesman: an official who makes out-of-bounds calls

passing: kicking the ball to a teammate

physical fitness: being in shape to play the game

punting: a kicking style used by goalies

referee: the official in charge of the game

save: when the goalie catches or blocks a ball from scoring

shooting: using your feet, body, or head to attempt to score a goal

sweeper: a fullback close to the goal used to assist other defenders

throw-in: throwing the ball back in play after it has gone out-of-bounds

trapping: using your body to stop a ball coming toward you in the air

warm-up: exercise to loosen up before practice or a game

wing: another name for left or right forward

World Cup: the world championship soccer tournament, held every four years

Appendix

Here is a list of leading U.S. soccer organizations. Write to them for more information about the sport:

United States Youth Soccer
Association
1835 Union Avenue – Suite 190
P.O. Box 18406
Memphis, TN 38104

American Youth Soccer
Organization
5403 West 138th Street
Box 5045
Hawthorne, CA 90251

United States Soccer Federation
National Headquarters
1750 East Boulder Street
Colorado Springs, CO 80909

Major Indoor Soccer League
7101 College Boulevard
Suite 320
Overland Park, KS 66210

Further Reading

Modern Soccer Superstars, by Bill Gutman (Dodd, Mead, 1979)

Our Soccer League, by Chuck Soloman (Crown, 1988)

Pelé—King of Soccer, by Claire and Frank Gault (Walker and Co., 1975)

Soccer Basics, by Alex Yannis (Prentice Hall, 1982)

Soccer For Juniors, by Robert Pollock (Scribner's, 1980)

Soccer For Young Champions, by Robert J. Antonacci and Anthony J. Puglisi (McGraw-Hill, 1978)

Soccer Fundamentals, by John Learmouth (St. Martin's, 1979)

About the Author

Marc Bloom writes on health, fitness, and sports for *The New York Times*, *Runner's World* magazine, and other publications. He lives in Marlboro, New Jersey, with his wife and two daughters, both of whom play soccer.

OTHER BOOKS BY MARC BLOOM
Cross-Country Running
The Marathon
Olympic Gold
The Runner's Bible

OTHER TITLES IN SERIES

FOOTBALL
BASKETBALL
BASEBALL

WIN A S⚽CCER BALL!

New series kickoff!

25 Winners!

Look for great books in the new **Know Your Game** series! You'll learn how to play all kinds of sports and win an official, regulation leather soccer ball — just like the ball the professionals use! Enter the KNOW YOUR GAME GIVEAWAY! Just fill in the coupon below and return it by November 30, 1990.

Rules: Entries must be postmarked by November 30, 1990. Winners will be picked at random and notified by mail. No purchase necessary. Void where prohibited. Taxes on prizes are the responsibility of the winners and their immediate families. Employees of Scholastic Inc.; its agencies, affiliates, subsidiaries; and their immediate families not eligible. For a complete list of winners, send a self-addressed stamped envelope to Know Your Game Giveaway, Giveaway Winners List, at the address provided below.

Fill in the coupon below or write the information on a 3" x 5" piece of paper and mail to: **KNOW YOUR GAME GIVEAWAY,** Scholastic Inc., P.O. Box 755, 730 Broadway, New York, NY 10003. Canadian residents send entries to: Iris Ferguson, Scholastic Inc., 123 Newkirk Road, Richmond Hill, Ontario, Canada L4C365.

- -

Know Your Game Giveaway

Name_____Age_____

Street _____

City_____State_____Zip _____

Where did you buy this *Know Your Game* book?

❏ Bookstore   ❏ Drugstore   ❏ Supermarket   ❏ Library

❏ Book Club   ❏ Book Fair   ❏ Other_____(specify)

KYG290